Ben's Teddy Bear

Story by Beverley Randell
Illustrated by Genevieve Rees

2

"Go to sleep, Ben,"
said Mom.

4

Look at Ben.

Ben is **not** asleep.

Ben is up!

"Mom, Mom!
Where is Teddy Bear?"

8

Mom is looking
for Teddy Bear.
Ben is looking
for Teddy Bear.

Where, oh where
is Teddy Bear?

12

"Here is Teddy Bear,"
said Mom.

"Thank you, Mom,"
said Ben.

14

"Go to sleep, Ben,"
said Mom.
"Go to sleep,
Teddy Bear."

Ben and Teddy Bear
are asleep.